SPEAKING

OF

RACE

Also by Patricia Roberts-Miller

Rhetoric and Demagoguery

Demagoguery and Democracy

Fanatical Schemes: Proslavery Rhetoric and the Tragedy of Consensus

Deliberate Conflict: Argument, Political Theory, and Composition Classes

Voices in the Wilderness: Public Discourse and the Paradox of the Puritan Rhetoric

SPEAKING OF RACE

How to Have Antiracist Conversations That Bring Us Together

PATRICIA ROBERTS-MILLER

NEW YORK

Speaking of Race: *How to Have Antiracist Conversations That Bring Us Together*

The Experiment, LLC
220 East 23rd Street, Suite 600
New York, NY 10010-4658
theexperimentpublishing.com

Library of Congress Cataloging-in-Publication Data

Names: Roberts-Miller, Patricia, 1959- author.
Title: Speaking of race : how to have antiracist conversations that bring us together / Patricia Roberts-Miller.
Description: New York : The Experiment, [2020] | Includes bibliographical references.
Identifiers: LCCN 2020046571 (print) | LCCN 2020046572 (ebook) | ISBN 9781615197323 (paperback) | ISBN 9781615197330 (ebook)
Subjects: LCSH: Racism. | Race. | Interpersonal communication.
Classification: LCC HT1521 .R6255 2021 (print) | LCC HT1521 (ebook) | DDC 305.8--dc23
LC record available at https://lccn.loc.gov/2020046571
LC ebook record available at https://lccn.loc.gov/2020046572

ISBN 978-1-61519-732-3
Ebook ISBN 978-1-61519-733-0

Cover and text design by Jack Dunnington

Manufactured in the United States of America

First printing January 2021
10 9 8 7 6 5 4 3 2 1

Contents

Part 1
Racism Is Hard to Talk About

1. *Why Do Disagreements About Racism Go So Badly?* 1

2. *Accusations of Racism as Acts of Respect and Kindness* 20

3. *It's Not About Intentions* 26

4. *Defining Racism* 37

Part 2
What to Say When Talking About Racism

5. *Assume Nothing* 49

6. *Listen* 54

7. *Consider Context* 67

8. *Think About Thinking* 70

9. *Understand the Role of Privilege* 75

10. *Don't Make the Discussion About You* 84

11. *Six Common Reasons People Say Something Is Racist* 91

12. *Racism Isn't About White People's Feelings* 116

13. *Key Things to Remember in the Heat of the Moment* 119

14. *A Final Note* 124

SUGGESTED READING 127

ACKNOWLEDGMENTS 133

ABOUT THE AUTHOR 134

Part 1

Racism Is Hard to Talk About

1
Why Do Disagreements About Racism Go So Badly?

On a scholarly mailing list–of communication scholars, no less–someone (call him Chester) posted a comment that some other people on the list thought was racist, and they said so. Chester pointed out his legitimate and impressive credentials of anti-racist work and, before long, was threatening to sue for defamation of character anyone who called him racist because, he said, calling someone a racist is such a terrible accusation. The argument got so ugly and unproductive that the mailing list shut down discussion altogether, about every topic.

This was the second time in a relatively short period that this list of communication scholars had been unable to have a productive disagreement about racism. The other controversy began with a disagreement as to whether the fact that a prestigious group was almost exclusively white was a sign that the selection processes were racist. In both cases, to say that the disagreement escalated quickly into accusations of bad faith and bad character is an understatement. It shot there like a rocket.

I knew about the controversies because I'm a professor of rhetoric—I have three degrees in rhetoric—and my area of expertise happens to be when rhetoric has disastrous consequences, when people talk themselves into bad decisions. And, in those decisions, racism is not infrequently a factor. In New York, Irish racism about the Italians meant that they wouldn't work together on mutually beneficial policies, or even have religious services together. To give a more drastic example, Hitler didn't take seriously that the United States might enter the war against Germany because he believed the US being a "mongrel" country (what we would call multiethnic and multicultural) meant its troops couldn't possibly be any good. That was a mistake he made because he was racist.

Not everyone who is racist is as racist as Hitler was (much of this book will be about the mistake of thinking of racism as an all-or-nothing situation), but some people are close enough, believing in and repeating evil, hateful, intentionally malicious racism. They're not basing their beliefs on reason, and their intentions aren't open to persuasion. This book isn't about trying to have constructive conversations with those people–let alone persuade them.*

Thinking about racism as all-or-nothing (you're Hitler or you "don't have a racist bone in your body") contributes to racism because

---

* Those people can't be persuaded, but they can be refuted, and that's worth doing under some circumstances. Adam Rutherford's *How to Argue With a Racist* is a useful resource for that endeavor. It's also sometimes a good choice not to engage them at all and just vote against them.

it enables us to refuse to think about whether we've done something racist on the grounds that we aren't as bad as Hitler. Thinking that "being racist" means "you're Hitler" means that we can't have useful disagreements about the various kinds of racism that don't immediately rise to genocide.

Still and all, why should a scholar and teacher of rhetoric be able to give useful advice about disagreements regarding racism? A lot of people think of rhetoric as the art of tricking people with words, what Protagoras, a fifth-century Athenian scholar of rhetoric, called the ability to make the worse argument seem as though it is the better. But rhetoric has also been called the art of understanding misunderstandings. This book is in that latter spirit–it's about understanding why people disagree so badly about racism, even scholars of communication, and how to learn from those disagreements and misunderstandings.

Certainly, disagreement is generally hard, and disagreements about racism do share some missteps with bad disagreements of all sorts. But the mailing list disagreements didn't just escalate–they escalated up exactly the same steps that bad disagreements about racism almost always do, whether the setting is social media, Thanksgiving dinner, a party, a meeting, and so on. The mailing list disagreements didn't go wrong just because digital disagreements are especially treacherous, nor was it that the people disagreeing didn't know how to disagree productively. This disagreement was among experts in rhetoric and communication–people who study disagreement for a living–yet it didn't go any better than nonexperts shouting at each other over pumpkin pie. The problem isn't how people disagree; it's about how people disagree when it comes to racism.

This book explains why disagreements about racism so often escalate in the same way. It's largely because so many people misunderstand what racism is and how it works; that is, what a disagreement about racism is really *about,* and what our options are when we disagree.

Imagine two people who disagree about whether the novel *To Kill a Mockingbird* is racist, Hubert and Emma. The conversation might be something like this:

> Hubert: "How can you like something as racist as *To Kill a Mockingbird* when the author was such a racist?"
>
> Emma: "How can you say that *To Kill a Mockingbird* is racist when the book explicitly condemns racism?"

Notice that both Hubert and Emma are taking the argument in a direction that can't really be answered–"how can you" do something? That is, they're making the issue about how it is that the other person can believe something so ridiculous. That's the first misstep in disagreeing about racism–making it about how stupid/misguided/ignorant the other person is for having the position they do.

There's something else interesting about how they're arguing, and it's especially clear if you look at it in terms of what Aristotle pointed out about how people argue on most issues. He pointed out that people tend to argue using what are called "enthymemes," basically compressed syllogisms. Instead of saying, "All men are mortal [major premise], and Socrates is a man [minor premise], and therefore Socrates is mortal [conclusion]," we say, "Of course Socrates will die [conclusion]–he's a man [minor premise]." The major premise (*all men are mortal*) is implied. If you look at the disagreement between Emma and Hubert that way, you can see that although they have very different conclusions, they both have minor premises that are factually true. Harper Lee was racist, and the book does condemn certain people as racist.

People often think that we disagree because we have different facts, or we disagree about the facts, or the other side doesn't have facts. On the contrary, as in the case of this argument, often, *we agree about the facts*. The disagreement is at the level of major premise. It's as though two people keep shouting at each other about whether Socrates is a man when they really disagree about whether all men are mortal. Hubert assumes that anything created by a racist is racist, and Emma doesn't. Emma assumes that a text can't condemn racism and be racist at the same time, and Hubert may or may not agree. They disagree about what the most useful criteria are for deciding that something is racist.

This book will start by talking about what are some ineffective ways to define racism before offering general advice about such disagreements. This book won't enable you to go through the world stamping things RACIST or NOT RACIST; it won't guarantee that you triumph over everyone who disagrees with you about whether something is racist, or ensure that you reach agreement any time the question of racism comes up. I can't give scripts that will always successfully persuade someone that they're racist or that you aren't, because there are too many ways a disagreement about racism might go. You may still find yourself in a lot of disagreements that end in neither person changing their mind, at least in the moment, but that might be a useful disagreement. You might also decide that you're interacting with someone incapable of rational argumentation, and this book will help you choose when to walk away. It will, I hope, help us often disagree *better* about racism, to have disagreements that, even if they end with us still disagreeing, at least leave us having learned something interesting and important.

One assumption we make about disagreements that make them unproductive is assuming that the only good outcome is for us to end up agreeing—that disagreement must end in persuasion. We also assume that a disagreement that results in someone getting angry is a bad disagreement. But a disagreement can be useful and helpful even if people end up angry and still disagreeing. In my experience, on big issues (and racism is always a big issue) we don't change our mind because of one conversation. A conversation about racism might move someone a small distance.

Or it might help us understand others better. Sometimes it will give us more empathy, so that we understand with compassion why there is disagreement. Understanding doesn't always mean empathy, though. It's useful for me to understand why my ceiling has water damage, but a better understanding of the damage doesn't make me more empathetic to the water damage. Racism is damaging, and understanding why someone is racist doesn't necessarily lead to being more empathetic to them.

Reducing racism in our world isn't a question of being nicer to racists so that they stop being racist, but it does mean understanding why racism seems to make sense to people and, often, why we don't see ourselves as racist, or recognize our actions as racist.

What's paradoxical about discussions about racism is that often everybody involved agrees that racism is bad, and that we shouldn't do or say racist things. We disagree about whether a particular thing is racist because we disagree about the best way to define "racist." That people disagree about a definition is pretty common; that's why in good disagreements we often have to take time to agree on a definition. In disagreements about racism, we too often skip that step. Disagreeing better means having more disagreements in which we first take the time to talk about the definition.

Imagine that you and I agree we'd like to watch a movie together, and I suggest a film you think is racist. Regardless of what movie we're talking about–*To Kill a Mockingbird, American Sniper, Big Trouble in Little China, Dances with Wolves*, or any one of the many movies about which this argument comes up–if you've made it known how you feel about my selection, there are, loosely, three ways the discussion is likely to go:

1. I can say, "Oh, OK, what would you like to watch?"
2. I can say, "Oh, I didn't know that–why do you think it's racist?"

3. I can decide that I know why you think it's racist, what you mean by "racist," what you think of me because you think I like a racist movie, and respond with something like, "It isn't racist; you're just too sensitive" or "How dare you call me racist?" or "It's just a movie" or various ways of refuting an argument I don't actually know you're making.

If I respond by cheerfully suggesting another movie, we don't talk about racism. Sometimes that's a fine choice (especially if I later try to seek out the best arguments I can find saying why the movie is racist). If I ask you why you think it's racist, *and I'm open to listening to your reasons*, we might have an interesting discussion, or I might listen to what you have to say and then say, "Interesting–well, what movie would you like to watch?" If I respond by rejecting your argument without even knowing what it is, then we may be shouting before too long, and there is a nonzero chance that one of us will call the other Hitler before storming off.

Disagreements about racism go wrong when I assume, without asking, that when you say a movie I suggested is racist it means that you think any of the following:

- I'm racist, since only racists like things that are racist.
- Racists are people who categorize everyone by race and are filled with an irrational hatred for everyone who isn't their race.
- Racists are so filled with hatred toward other races that they intentionally try to hurt members of other races at every opportunity.
- Racism is bad because it comes from those bad intentions and hatred, and it's harmful because it hurts the feelings of individuals of those other races.

- I should spend my life filled with shame and guilt for being racist (or for being the race I am).

In other words, I'm assuming that racist acts are what racists do, and racism is about the feelings and intentions of racist individuals, and how the intentional acts of racism hurt other individuals, and the reason to call someone racist is to make sure they wallow in shame for the rest of the life. That isn't a useful way to think about racism.

I hope to persuade people that liking or saying something racist doesn't necessarily mean that you are a horrible and hateful person who should wear sackcloth and ashes forever, depending on what it is, what makes it racist, how racist it is, why you like it, and how you respond once you understand the criticism. In the words of the *Avenue Q* song, "we're all a little bit racist," so we are all going to be told at some point that we've said or done something racist, and sometimes it will be true.

Sometimes it won't. Sometimes people aren't a little bit racist, but very racist, and some people are evil, and some people should feel ashamed. But even in the circumstances in which we've said or done something so racist that we should feel shame about it, our feeling shame is not a useful end to the disagreement (nor is it the goal). The end goal of conversations about racism should be about how we strive together to live in a less racist world. We can't do that unless we're all willing to hear that we've said, done, liked, or enabled something racist.

We disagree about whether something is racist because we disagree about how to define "racist." Going to the dictionary won't help, since dictionaries provide common usage, and if, as is the case with "racist," common usage is troubled, it won't provide a definition that will solve our problem. Dictionaries often define "racist" as a belief that "race" determines human capacity.* But, believing that "race" has no impact on

* See, for instance, merriam-webster.com/dictionary/racist.

what a person is capable of achieving is actually racist–it dismisses institutional racism. Sometimes people emphasize hostility, or insist that it's only racism if we're talking about "biological" races rather than culture (although the notion of race as a biological category is fairly recent), or make "racist" such an extreme stance that it applies to no one other than Hitler.

So, this book is largely about what are more and less useful definitions of racism, and I'll argue for what I think is a useful way to define it–one that emphasizes harm. But nobody died and made me Webster. Every conversation about whether something (an act, policy, statement, movie, etc.) is racist should begin by agreeing on a definition of "racism." If we can't agree on that, then that's the place the disagreement will stay: What are better and worse ways to define racism?

The question is: What are we trying to *do* when we disagree about whether something is racist? If we're trying to purify the world of racist people because they're bad people, then it begins as a conversation about extermination. And we're talking about motives, intent, and identity. But if we're trying to reduce racism because it's harmful, then we're talking about actions, systems, practices, and what damage they do. That's where I think the conversation is more useful.

A lot of people say that they're afraid to talk about race at all because they're afraid of being called racist. The political scientists Jeffrey M. Berry and Sarah Sobieraj say that this concern is particularly high among conservatives because they have been accused of being racist. They quote a survey respondent ("Missy") who describes regretting posting something on social media that prompted several of her friends to call her racist: "Being called racist is a really powerful insult."* That was what Chester (the very liberal communication professor) said. There are a few points about Chester and

---

* See Jeffrey M. Berry and Sarah Sobieraj, *The Outrage Industry: Political Opinion Media and the New Incivility* (New York: Oxford University Press, 2014), 145.

Missy that are striking. First, despite what Berry and Sobieraj seem to suggest, being called racist isn't restricted to conservatives–it happened to Chester, after all. Later in the book I'll mention times I was told I'd done something racist (I had). Noel Ignatiev, a scholar of racism, is supposed to have said that our culture is so racist that it isn't even possible to talk about racism without saying something racist.

Second, both Chester and Missy were more concerned about having been called racist than they were concerned that they might have said something racist (they had). Instead of trying to be open to criticism of what they said, they both focused on their own feeling of having been called a horrible human being. And that's the third point that's striking. They shared an understanding of what it means to be accused of having done something racist: It's an accusation that you are a horrible person. They believed, like many people, that being told you said something racist is *really* saying you're a monster.

As Ta-Nehisi Coates says, "The word *racist* ... conjures, if not a tobacco-spitting oaf, then something just as fantastic–an orc, troll, or gorgon."* And, then, the person called racist becomes obsessed with "personal exoneration," so that we can't talk about whether what was said was racist, and that's what we should be talking about. Ibram X. Kendi says, "racist" "is not the worst word in the English language; it is not the equivalent of a slur. It is descriptive, and the only way to undo racism is to consistently identify and describe it–and then dismantle it."† Because neither Chester nor Missy were open to thinking about whether they had a racist belief (because they were so focused on having been called a racist), they didn't dismantle their own racism.

---

* See Ta-Nehisi Coates, *Between the World and Me* (New York: Spiegel & Grau, 2015), 97.

†See Kendi, *How to Be an Antiracist*, 9.

2
Accusations of Racism as Acts of Respect and Kindness

In some of the classes I teach, I have to explain the concept of a "social construct"—those are things, like money or geopolitical borders, that only exist because we agree they exist. National borders are where they are because enough people with the right kind of power agreed that's where the border will be. People might have previously agreed to put it somewhere else; it might be somewhere else later because people agree it should be moved. Geopolitical borders aren't objective in the way that, say, gravity is—it exists whether we recognize it or not. But they aren't subjective either. They have real consequences, as anyone can say who finds themselves on the wrong side of a border in terms of services, safety, or taxes.

In one class I used the example of "whiteness" and pointed out that "white" is a socially constructed (and not biological) category. In the US, for instance, Catholics weren't white for much of the nineteenth century, Jews weren't white until well into the twentieth century (and many people still don't consider them white), Italians and Poles weren't considered white until halfway through the twentieth century (and the prevalence of "Polack" jokes suggests perhaps even longer). I mentioned that the N-word was often used for people from India, North Africa, the Middle East, and even the Irish until at least the early twentieth century.

One of the African American students in the class walked with me back to my office because, he said, he thought what I'd said in class was racist. We proceeded to have a really confusing conversation before he persuaded me that he was completely right. And he was. The conversation was confusing because he was trying to persuade me that Irish Americans were never treated as badly as African Americans, and I agreed with him—that's simply a fact. While factory work was bad, it was never as bad as slavery, and that's why slaves tried to escape to places where they might have to work in factory. There weren't a lot of factory workers risking their lives in order to become slaves, after all. The conversation was confusing because I was being obtuse. What he knew, and I didn't, was there was a racist narrative that the Irish Americans and African Americans were equally badly treated in the nineteenth century, and so the fact that the Irish "pulled themselves up" showed that the African Americans could have, but didn't. Therefore, current disparities are the consequence of "Black culture" that thwarts success in various ways (this narrative is what is sometimes called "cultural racism"). He thought I had been endorsing that racist narrative, and, to be honest, everything I had said in class could be interpreted as my having done so. He correctly interpreted what I said, although he was wrong about my intent.

Irish Americans were never treated as badly as African Americans (for starters, there was not a massive economic market of buying and selling Irish Americans), and they were reclassified as white because it was politically useful for the Jacksonian Democrats to do so. The Jacksonian Democrats wanted to preserve slavery and couldn't get the votes to do that unless they got a group outside of the openly pro-slavery states to vote with them. So, they made the classic move of creating what's called a "wedge" issue. That's an issue that will break apart groups that might be aligned. Jacksonian Democrats used race as a wedge to separate Irish Americans and African Americans. They deliberately fomented racism in the Irish American community about African Americans, while reducing racism against

Irish Americans by including them in political leadership.*

I never meant to promote the argument that the success of the Irish is evidence that there's something wrong with African Americans, because that's an argument that is absurd on its face (and, at the time, I didn't even know anyone made that argument). I still cringe when I think about this interaction because I was *so* clueless, but he stuck with me.

Eventually, he connected the dots for me, but it took him a long time to get there, and he took that time. And I remain grateful to him that he did so. And, eventually, he understood that I didn't intend to endorse that narrative. But, we both knew that what I'd done in class was racist, even if I didn't have that intention. The fact is that if there were other students who believed that racist narrative, they would feel confirmed by what I said in class. What I

---

* For more on this topic, see Noel Ignatiev's *How the Irish Became White* (New York and London: Routledge, 1995).

had done was racist, and I needed to undo the damage. He wasn't asking me to cover myself in shame, apologize profusely, wear a hair shirt. What he and I both wanted was for me to go into the next class and clarify the point about the Irish. And it's what I've done ever since. His calling my behavior racist made me a better teacher.

Someone telling you that you've done something racist can be an act of respect and kindness. In a culture as racist as ours, and given the long history of racism, it's impossible not to say or do something racist from time to time. Someone pointing out our racism gives us a chance to do something useful about that culture and history.

3
It's Not About Intentions

Racism can be built into systems even without there being any individuals who have the conscious intent to be racist. Think about this in terms of how some people are physically excluded from some older buildings because the buildings are anti-accessible. I teach in a building that was designed to have heavy doors that are hard to open, stairs all over the place (often just for aesthetics), a ramp that is much too steep, one small elevator that doesn't go to one of the floors (where some instructors have office hours). The building was designed such that anyone who used a wheelchair, scooter, or even crutches or a cane was physically excluded. That exclusion was probably not conscious on the part of the architects or builders, but it was a manifestation of the beliefs at the time about what sorts of bodies were imagined to be part of the university community. There was no good reason to exclude people in wheelchairs and so on–they were perfectly capable of contributing to the university as much as anyone, except for the ways the university structures and institutional practices excluded them from doing so. That kind of cruel and unnecessary exclusion was the consequence of a sort of bigotry that is so widespread that participating in it doesn't require conscious thought–it can rely on thoughtlessness.

We are in a new era, and my university has done a lot of work to renovate the building, but there are still those stairs, that small elevator and unsafe ramps. That exclusion, and the physical barriers to success, hurt more than just feelings. Students, staff, faculty, and visitors to the building face physical obstructions to their being able to get to class, work, meetings, office hours, and events on time, and sometimes even at all. It's harder for them to succeed. The exclusion of the building hurts everyone (albeit to different degrees) because it means that staff and faculty can't do their jobs as well, students can't contribute as much to class. We lose the voices of people who are physically prevented from being part of our community.

So, what should we do?

Is the solution to this problem of exclusion for people to be consumed with shame and guilt? Not really. The people who designed the building are probably long dead; the people who use the building now feeling shame wouldn't make the building any more accessible. It's useful for people not inconvenienced by the building's failings to recognize the advantage they have as the primary act for working on practices and policies that would solve that problem of exclusion. The goal is inclusion, and shame is, at best, a way to motivate people to prioritize inclusion.

Whether the exclusion was intentional or not doesn't change the reality that the building is exclusive; it was designed to exclude people, even if unconsciously or thoughtlessly. We live and work within figurative structures that were designed to be racist, perhaps consciously, perhaps unconsciously—the intentions of the designers don't change the reality that the design is racist. The end goal of activism about accessibility is not to make those without disabilities feel shame and guilt; it's to motivate people to make the university more accessible. Indifference is as much a problem as hatred.

The most extreme manifestation of racism is genocide, and genocide happens not just because of the people who hate, but because of the people who don't care. As Ian Kershaw, a prominent historian of Nazi Germany, famously said, "The road to Auschwitz was built by hate, but paved with indifference."* People can engage in racism by failing to object to racism.

The notion that racism is always and only the consequence of people who plan to be racist doesn't make sense. As Ijeoma Oluo says, racism is not

> the work of a bunch of random white people waking up each morning and saying to themselves, "Today I will do what I can to oppress a person of color." . . . We cannot look at a society where racial inequity is so universal and longstanding and say, "This is all the doing of a few individuals with hate in their hearts." It just doesn't make sense.†

When racism is built into the system, racist actions and policies don't require a conscious

---

* *Popular Opinion and Political Dissent in the Third Reich: Bavaria 1933–1945* (Oxford, England: Clarendon Press, 1983)

†See page 31 in *So You Want to Talk About Race* (New York: Seal Press, Hachette Book Group, 2018).

intention to do harm on the part of individuals, let alone hatred. We won't solve racism if we only focus on the conscious intentions of individuals, or even their feelings.

Because "am I racist?" is what cognitive psychologists call a "hot cognition" question–that is, it triggers a strong emotional reaction–this book will often make points about racism through analogies that aren't about racism. Bear with me on that. By using a low-stakes example to make a point about how people think, and then showing how that particular way people think plays out when it comes to racism, I'm not equating the low-stakes situation and racism. It's a strategy I've found helpful in teaching (not just me–I stole it from Aristotle). It's hard to look at something a new way if hot cognition has been triggered, so it makes sense to try to talk about the principles in regard to low-stakes topics, and then move over to the high-stakes one.

For instance, Missy and Chester both said something that some people thought was racist, and the question quickly became focused on whether *they* were racist. Let's step away from that high-stakes example. Imagine that we're roommates, and I let dishes sit in the sink for days. You can make it an issue of who I am ("You're a selfish pig for leaving dishes in the sink") or what I'm doing ("Hey, I really need you to get to the dishes the same day"). If you make our disagreement about that first issue, what would it mean to "win" the argument? You'd succeed in persuading me that I'm an awful human being, and your "success" might actually reduce the chances of my doing the dishes more often. After all, if your goal in the disagreement is to persuade me to do the dishes, persuading me that my basic identity is that of a jerk gives me no place for improvement–it's hopeless. I'm basically a terrible person. If we keep the disagreement not on the issue of my worthiness as a human being but rather on the dishes, then we've got a lot of possible options for solving the problem–I could pay for a maid, pay you to do the dishes, do all the cooking, clean out the litter box, set an alarm to remind myself. If the problem is that I'm a horrible person, then it's a hopeless problem; if the problem is something I'm doing, I can be hopeful about finding a solution. Keeping the issue on actions and not identity is more likely to enable us to solve the problem.

If you persuade me that I'm a racist and I think being a racist means that I'm a monster, then I'm just left in a world of self-loathing and I'm not any less racist–or any less likely to do racist things. If you persuade me that I've said or done something racist, then I can stop saying or doing that thing: not because this conversation should be framed in terms of actions rather than identities out of concern for being nice to racists–or even being particularly careful about the feelings of people doing racist things–but because it's a more productive conversation to have overall.

In an advice column about workplaces that I often read, there was a long and fascinating comment thread in which people were sharing stories about times that very nice coworkers were using terms, avatars, or emojis that had sexual, scatological, or racist meanings of which they were unaware. One generally sweet person, for instance, was using as an avatar an image that she liked because it was an animal she really liked, but she didn't know that it had been co-opted by the nastiest kind of white supremacist. There was no doubt that she didn't know that, so the puzzle was how to tell her without sending her into a shame spiral. She never *meant* to appear to be endorsing an extremely racist group. But people who didn't know her, especially customers, would assume that she (and therefore her company) was endorsing white supremacist groups and ideology. She didn't intend to convey a racist message, but she did.

We can be racist without intending to. When it comes to having said or done something racist, that it was unintentional is not a "get out of racism free" card.

Imagine that I hit your car, and you wanted me to pay for the damage I did. Would you decide that I hadn't actually hit your car if I didn't intend to? You might be less mad at me, it might change your opinion on whether I'm a bad person, but it wouldn't change anything about the damage to your car. Similarly, whether I intended to do something racist is relevant to the question of whether I'm a bad person, but it doesn't change whether I did something damaging.

If I hit your car, it wouldn't help solve the problem of your damaged car for you to leap out and yell at me that I'm a bad driver–even if that's true–because raising the issue of my being a good driver means that it would appear relevant for me to show you my excellent results on the driving test, my good insurance score, affidavits from people who say they saw me drive well once. Just as it's more productive to begin the conversation about your car with, "Hey, I think you hit my car" instead of "You're a bad driver because you just hit my car," it's more productive to start the conversation about racism with, "Hey, I think that was a racist thing to say" rather than, "You're a racist because you said that thing." It's also useful to try to hear "that was a racist thing" rather than "I'm racist."

Jay Smooth has a really useful video* about how we shouldn't argue about whether someone is racist, but about whether someone did something racist, and he points out that, if someone stole his wallet, he would chase the person down, not to persuade them they're a thief, but to get his wallet back.

---

* See "How to Tell Someone They Sound Racist" on YouTube.

4
Defining Racism

Racism is a particularly damaging form of a natural cognitive bias—what's called "in-group favoritism." Humans have a tendency to think of our world as in-group (not necessarily the group that is in power, but the group we're in) versus *others*. Some of those *others* are neutral, but some are out-groups—that is, groups we define ourselves against, that we take pride in *not* being. We can feel good about ourselves simply because we are *not* them (this plays into implicit racism in all sorts of interesting ways).

In- and out-groups can be oddly meaningless and meaningful at the same time.

So, for instance, if I'm trying to sell you a new car, you'll trust me more if I share your birthday, say, or first or last name, or place of birth, even though those characteristics have nothing to do with whether it's a good car, or whether I'm a trustworthy salesperson. I could also increase your trust of me by taking some time to bond with you about a shared enemy–Libras, Aggies, Bears fans–although, again, that shared enemy doesn't actually mean anything about the quality of the car or my goodwill toward you. It's meaningless.

But it will *seem* meaningful.

We have a tendency to see the in-group as varied and diverse, with complicated inner lives and motives, but out-group members are all the same. In other words, we treat bad behavior as an exception just for the in-group, and not for any of our out-groups. If a Texan (an in-group for me) behaves badly, then I'll find reasons to explain their behavior as not representative of the whole group (#notallTexans), but if a member of an out-group (car salespeople) behaves badly, I'll think, "Typical." Bad behavior *means* something different depending on whether it's on the part of in- or out-group members.

Racism is that tendency to see in- and out-groups as meaningful and explanatory, but, instead of recognizing that "racial" groups are often arbitrary (such as sharing a birthday) or social constructs (such as being a Texan), it says that the imagined (and often projected) group characteristics are Real—they're grounded in biology, genetics, or culture (that is, racial groups are *essentially* different, different down to their very essence).* Racism is the tendency to favor our "racial" in-group in how we think, vote, hire, tell stories. It's useful to characterize this kind of essentialism as racism specifically when that in-group favoritism reinforces existing inequalities. I've come to define racism this way:

* For a particularly effective discussion of what's wrong with biological/genetic racism, see *How to Argue With a Racist.*

> *Something (an act, a system, a policy, a movie) is racist to the extent that it appeals to or reinforces (explicitly or implicitly, consciously or unconsciously) essentialized perceptions of "racial" groups in any way that strengthens existing political, economic, or cultural inequalities.*

There are other ways of defining racism, but this one seems to me useful for reasons that should become clear in the course of this book. For instance, by this definition, a policy can be racist without that being the deliberate goal of the people who proposed or enacted it. If a policy disproportionately harms a racial group, it's the damage that matters–it's racist. That the harm was unintentional doesn't change the harm.

Because we are in a culture with political inequalities, because in-group favoritism is a natural cognitive bias, it's extremely unlikely that our biases can be entirely free of our cultural categories of "race." We're all at least a little bit racist. The fact that in-group favoritism is natural doesn't mean it's OK–it's natural to want to take anger out on innocent bystanders, but the fact that it's a natural impulse isn't justification. Depending on our temperament, we might have a stronger or weaker desire to take our anger out on others, and it might be extremely difficult for some people to keep from having that desire, but we can keep ourselves from engaging in the action, and can rectify any harm we do if our restraint fails. It's the same with our impulses to judge through a racist lens, even if unconsciously. The harm in racist actions is not that they come from racist impulses or feeling, but in what they do to others, and to our shared world.

Paradoxically, focusing on feelings can make us *more* comfortable saying racist things, as long as we don't think we're hurting the feelings of anyone around us. I have several friends who have a parent (or two) from Mexico who describe a similar puzzling interaction. They don't fit the racist stereotype of "Mexican," and so they have often found themselves in a social setting where people are talking trash about "Mexicans." If they object to the racism without revealing that their "friends" are insulting them, then they get called "politically correct" and the "friends" double down on their racist claims, saying something like, "Well, you know it's true." If they reveal that they're in the group the "friends" are attacking, then those people apologize. But those people don't apologize for thinking the racist thing, or for saying it, but for saying it *in front of them*.*

Those two responses–your criticism of what we're saying can be dismissed because you aren't directly hurt by what we're saying,

---

* Trevor Noah describes the same kind of experience growing up in South Africa, as when a shopkeeper said something racist in front of Noah and his mother, thinking they couldn't understand Afrikaans. When Noah's mother made it clear they spoke Afrikaans, the shopkeeper, as Noah says, "didn't apologize for being racist; he merely apologized for aiming his racism at us." See page 55 in *Born a Crime: Stories from a South African Childhood* (New York: Random House, 2016) for more on this.

or we're not sorry for thinking it but for saying it in front of you–seem sensible if we think of the harm of racism as hurting the feelings of individuals of that race. Thinking of racism that way seems to suggest that as long as we don't hurt their feelings by being racist in front of them, we're all good.

But racism isn't just feelings; it's a set of beliefs. It's about beliefs that *that* race is more criminal, lazier, less American, more dishonest, more prone to terrorism. The problem isn't that these friends said something racist in front of people of that race; it's that they believe those racist things. Believing that "Mexicans" are more criminal, lazy, prone to drug use, or whatever particular stereotype was behind the comments my friends had to hear isn't something that *only* manifests itself in comments made when people think there are no "Mexicans" around. People who expect that everyone around them will agree that "Mexicans" are criminal will take that belief into a jury, voting booth, hiring committee, admissions committee. And they may not be aware they're making a decision on the basis of race. They'll think they're being rational.

I'm occasionally mistaken for Jewish, which I've discovered when people have tried to make me feel bad by flinging an anti-Semitic slur at me. What they did is wrong, but not because they made me feel bad about being Jewish, since that isn't something I can do. Their saying things to me was bad, but it would have been just as bad had they never said those things out loud–what was (and is) wrong is that they have *beliefs* about Jews that mean they will make personal and political decisions based on their sense of Jews as a dangerous out-group.

To frame the problem of racism as though it is a question of individual feelings (racists feel hostility, and the victims feel offended) misses the whole point of *our shared world* being damaged by racism. Falsely framing the harm of racism as what it does to individuals' feelings makes it seem as though the only people who can legitimately object to racism are the members of the group mentioned in the racism. And that is the origin of the "You're just a social justice warrior" attempt to redirect the more important question of whether what I said was racist to your motives for objecting. Paradoxically, if I succeed in deflecting the conversation away from your criticism to my feelings, I fail at resolving the question of whether I've said or done something racist. Maybe I have, and maybe I haven't, but I'll never know without hearing what you have to say.

Part 2

What to Say When Talking About Racism

5
Assume Nothing

There's a guy who is often next to me on the bikes at the gym, and he only watches one network. While there was a political controversy going on about immigration, I was struck by how often the "crawler" (the horizontal bar at the bottom of the screen) had news about the arrest of undocumented Latinx. Sometimes the crimes were violent, and sometimes not, and there appeared to be little or no follow-up (such as whether charges were dropped, or the person was convicted). The incidents were from all over the country, and they had nothing in common except that the person accused was an undocumented Latinx. That piling up of instances would leave a viewer with the impression that undocumented Latinx are constantly committing crime.

And then I understood a disagreement I'd had with several people on social media about crime and immigration. They were insistent that undocumented immigrants were responsible for a tremendous amount of crime, but they couldn't cite any data other than their own certainty. I tried citing research from various sites showing that undocumented workers are, if anything, more likely to be victims of crimes than perpetrators. I even cited research from the Cato Institute, a conservative think tank, that concluded that homicide conviction rate for undocumented immigrants "was 16 percent below that of native-born Americans in Texas in 2015," and the conviction rates were "7.9 percent and 77 percent below that of native-born Americans for sex crimes and larceny, respectively."*

I got nowhere. When I saw that crawler, and thought about what the rhetorical impact would be of an almost endless number of individual instances, I realized those people on social media probably got their information from that same network. It would be persuasive.

We live in the world of stories about our experiences. If all the stories we have about bears show them to be friendly, an unfriendly bear will seem to be the exception. The friendly bear stereotype would be more easily accessible than the unfriendly bear stereotype. That belief about bears can be created by fiction (movies, TV shows, cartoons, novels) and yet have consequences for our behavior in the real world–we might try to approach a bear

---

* See Alex Nowrasteh, "Criminal Immigrants in Texas in 2017: Illegal Immigrant Conviction Rates and Arrest Rates for Homicide, Sex Crimes, Larceny, and Other Crimes," Cato Institute, Immigration Research and Policy Brief no. 13 (August 2019).

in the wild, or try to pose with it for a photo. That TV network tells a lot of stories about crime, and, if the majority of them are ones in which undocumented Latinx have committed the crime, it would leave viewers with a ratio of Latinx to non-Latinx crime stories that would make Latinx seem overwhelmingly criminal. They would feel as though they have direct experience that shows the studies I was citing to be false.

It doesn't require watching that network to have false narratives that come from fiction. At some point, I realized that I was strongly committed to a stereotype about how defense expert witnesses function in trials, and I wondered why I did. I'd never read any studies on the issue, and I'd never talked to the trial attorneys I know about it. I realized I had this stereotype about defense expert witnesses because of how they are consistently presented in shows like *Law & Order*. The brain knows that it has examples; it doesn't necessarily categorize those examples on the basis of source. I thought I had lots of examples of how expert witnesses behave, but I actually only had lots of stories from a TV show.

They're just stories.

6
Listen

Rational argumentation is about two things:

1. Can you identify the evidence that would cause you to change your mind?
2. Do you really believe your major premise?

Racism violates both of these rules. Racist claims are nonfalsifiable, and they don't hold to major premises across groups. So, one way to know whether your belief about some group is racist is to ask yourself if it's falsifiable, and if it's grounded in a major premise that applies across all groups.

We are fulfilling at least one criterion of being racist when we treat another group as essentially so different from us that we feel we are justified in holding them to different standards from the ones to which we hold our in-group. That's a little complicated, so I'll try to be more clear. If I refuse to buy products from Boy Scouts, and I say it's because they knock on my door, but I buy products from Girl Scouts who also knock on my door, you'd be justified in pointing out that my position isn't rational. I'm not actually refusing to buy from the Boy Scouts for knocking on my door. That's just a useful excuse for my acting on the basis of a stereotype about Boy Scouts that I'm refusing to bring into the realm of argument.

If you point out that Girl Scouts also knock on the door, and I don't change my position, then knocking on the door was an example of why I don't like Boy Scouts. It wasn't a reason.

And that's how racism works. Our "evidence" for our claims doesn't operate the same way across race. Imagine that someone argues that Black men are racially more criminal, as is shown by their higher incarceration rates (a common argument). It's true that African Americans are disproportionately represented in prisons. But, if that fact shows a *biological* or *essential* criminality in Black men, then the fact that white males are disproportionately likely to commit white-collar crimes must mean that white men have a *biological* or *essential* propensity for fraud. If correlation equals causation when it comes to African American males, then it has to do the same when it comes to white males—otherwise, it's a racist argument.

Someone committed to the narrative that African Americans are essentially more criminal is likely to engage in the kind of "confirmation bias" that enables us to make exceptions for in-group members. When someone in our in-group does something wrong, we explain it via external factors ("White men commit more white-collar crime because they're more likely to be in situations where that's an option"), but internal or essential factors if they're out-group ("African American men are more likely to commit crimes because they are [or their culture is] essentially criminal"). A non-racist explanation would explain them both in the same way—either it's external factors or internal factors.*

A person who explains things differently dependent on race doesn't necessarily *mean*

* Since prisons are overwhelmingly filled with people who have committed drug offenses, the disproportionate prison population might be the result of disparate arrest practices. As one study shows, "Blacks are no more likely than whites to use illicit drugs or be involved in drug sales; consequently, these behaviors do not explain disparities in arrest rates." Ferrer, Barbara, and John M. Connolly. "Racial Inequities in Drug Arrests: Treatment in Lieu of and After Incarceration" in *American Journal of Public Health* 108, no. 8 (2018): 968–69. For more on racism and arrest/conviction rates, see Michelle Alexander, *The New Jim Crow* (New York: The New Press, 2020), as well as the September 2020 Harvard Law School Criminal Justice Policy Program Study, "Racial Disparities in the Massachusetts Criminal System."

to do that; they may not even be aware that they are. However, the fact that they are explaining the same kind of thing differently, and that the difference is favorable to one race and unfavorable to another–that makes it a racist explanation.

Racism isn't about a mustache-twirling villain who says we should kill this group because we hate them. Racism is about how people unconsciously treat one another, make decisions (about hiring, voting, viewing), and fail to act because we believe, on the basis of all the examples we've been given, that "those people" are not people who we should treat as we would want to be treated. If I have a strong stereotype about an out-group race, and I refuse to look at good arguments showing that I might be wrong, then my belief is racist.

It's a basic human failing that we attribute good outcomes to our individual agency. If we win at cards–even a more or less random game–we believe that we won as a consequence of our skill; if we lose, it was random chance. If we get a good outcome consistently, we are likely to say it is the consequence of choices we have made, rather than other factors, such as race.

I was reading a comment thread on an advice column (I love advice columns), and the columnist mentioned something about race. And the comment thread turned into a perfect gem of how not to think about race.

The question had to do with whether someone should call the police on a problematic neighbor, and the columnist had advised caution if the neighbor was a POC. Some people argued that the advice columnist had made it an issue of racism by bringing up the issue of race. This is a way of thinking about the power of language that has fascinated me for years–something doesn't exist until you name it. A racist relative can spew racism all over the Thanksgiving table, but you're racist for saying they're racist? Because you're the one who said the word *racist*? That's like thinking that no one has cancer till the doctor says it's cancer, and so the doctor's the one who caused the cancer. Or that, although your uncle was being verbally abusive to someone, there wasn't a conflict until someone called him out. An act, belief, statement, movie, etc. can be racist without ever mentioning the word *race*, just as a person can have cancer without anyone saying that word.

But here was my favorite comment about the advice columnist's advice to think carefully about how race might play into calling the police. In the thread about whether it was reasonable to think that people of color are treated differently from white people by the police, someone wrote a comment that began: "I'm a sixty-year-old white woman, and I've never had any problems with the police." As it happens, when I read that comment, I was a sixty-year-old white woman, and it's appalling the things I've done that didn't get me a ticket. When I was a sixteen- to eighteen-year-old white woman in an area patrolled by the Torrance Police Department, I never got a ticket, even though in at least two cases I really should have. But both times the cops let it go.

Meanwhile, however, a Latino friend got pulled over all the time, including for going one mile an hour over the speed limit. No kidding. I had a friend who appeared Latino and was falsely accused of having an open container in the vehicle (one that the officer had put into the car).

At another point, I had a commute that involved a lot of time on a road that had a ludicrously low speed limit. Everyone drove fifteen to twenty miles over the speed limit, including me, old people, young people, people trailering tractors. It was patrolled, and so I sometimes sailed past the police egregiously speeding, and I was never pulled over. I did see people pulled over by the police–and they were always and only young Black males.

So, I assumed that this woman would say the same thing I would, that, as a sixty-year-old white woman with POC friends, I can say that police are much more a threat to my friends than they are to me. I have been pulled over by police, always with justification, but I've never been given a ticket. So, when I read a comment that began, "I'm a sixty-year-old white woman, and I've never had a problem with the police," I thought this comment would go on to acknowledge that police treat white women differently, that we've seen our POC friends (or friends who even look POC) treated completely differently from the treatment to which we are accustomed.

And, yes, I'm always polite to the police. I keep my hands in clear view, make sure the officers can see that I'm not reaching for a weapon, and defer to them endlessly. But so did my friends. So do lots of people. And some of them get tickets for going one mile over the speed limit, or have a rusty beer can thrown into their car, or get shot. So, my experience as a sixty-year-old white woman is that my interactions with the police are wildly different from people who aren't (or don't present as) white. My experience shows that our culture's policing is perniciously racist.

Instead, she said that her experience as a white sixty-year-old woman was proof that POC have nothing to fear from the police. She said that she was respectful, and that's why she had never had a bad experience with the police. It was attributing to her behavior something that was a consequence of her race. It was racist.

It's completely missing the point. *It isn't listening*. It's a circular argument that unintentionally proves the point that people of different races have different experiences with the police. Her argument is that being respectful to the police is why she's had good experiences, while not acknowledging the large number of people of color who were respectful and got shot. She almost certainly doesn't know about them. I only started to pay attention to the disparate treatment of the police because I happened to have close friends who were or appeared to be people of color. I noticed who was pulled over on that road because I was working on a hypothesis (to which I remain committed) that bad drivers drive with hats on.

That you have never seen something doesn't mean it doesn't exist. That something is not in my world of experience doesn't mean it isn't in anyone else's. I am a height for which theater and airplane seats are fine. That doesn't mean that people who are much taller and say that they can't be comfortable simply need to be polite to the ticket taker or flight attendant and they will have my experience.

Michael Eric Dyson describes being pulled over by a police officer in front of the seminary where Dyson taught. When Dyson said he was a professor at that seminary, the officer responded, "Sure, and I'm John Wayne."[*] I've never had a police officer doubt me when I said I was a professor. Dyson describes an incident in which his son was nearly arrested simply because he wouldn't admit to something he hadn't done[†]; as with my Roma friend, the officer escalated the interaction. An African American friend brought her teenage son to work one day during spring break, and he left the office to use the restroom. He didn't return for some time, so she went looking for him. She found him being detained by a campus police officer for no reason the officer could explain. My friend's arrival did nothing to calm the situation, which the officer was escalating. It wasn't until an administrator (a white woman) showed up that anyone was able to persuade the officer to back off.

---

* See page 12 in *Tears We Cannot Stop: A Sermon to White America* (New York: St. Martin's Press, 2017).

†Ibid., pp. 27–31.

That a white person has consistently good experiences with police is not proof that the problem is whether people are respectful–it's evidence that policing is racist.

7
Consider Context

In the nineteenth century, especially in England, there was significant discrimination against Irish Catholics. In the US, it took the form of serious arguments about whether Catholics should be allowed to vote, intermittent anti-Catholic riots, and even an anti-Catholic political party, and it was grounded in stereotypes about the Irish being incapable of democratic citizenship because they were mindlessly faithful to the Pope, culturally criminal, politically corrupt, drags on social welfare systems, terrorists plotting an overthrow of democracy, basically drunks, and too fecund. In the US, racism against the Irish declined when the Jacksonian Democrats found them a politically useful bloc. I was surprised to learn that there are still traces of that anti-Irish culture, such as, oddly enough, in the conventional representation of clowns. In the nineteenth and early twentieth centuries there was the racist stereotype of Irish, sometimes called "Stage Irish" (that is, how they were portrayed on stage): with red hair and plaids, they were clearly Irish, and with a red nose and staggering gait, they were clearly drunk. Conventional representations of clowns in many areas (including the US) have their origin in the Stage Irish, with the additional joke of the clown car–that there is an apparently endless number of them. So, for a time, clowns would have been funny partially because people enjoyed laughing at the Irish, and the behavior of clowns would have reinforced harmful stereotypes about the Irish, the specific stereotypes that fueled discrimination against them. Does that mean that clowns are racist?

Clowns were harmful as long as "the Irish" were a culturally, economically, and politically marginalized out-group, since clowns reinforced the dominant stereotypes about the Irish that contributed to their marginalization. But, as the Irish became white, and thereby became part of the majority's in-group, clowns became less damaging–there wasn't a dominant and harmful stereotype for them to reinforce. And, after a time, clowns weren't even recognized as Irish. They don't do the harm they once did, at least not in the US, so I don't think it's useful to call them racist, and there's no need to ban or even change the conventional representation of clowns. Because a racist stereotype is harmful to the extent that it reinforces existing harm, the same movie, joke, or action could be racist in one situation or era and not in another.

8
Think About Thinking

A friend, whose father's family is ethnically Norwegian, tells a funny story about one of her aunts. Her aunt had lived for most of her life in an ethnically diverse part of Chicago, and loved it, getting along with everyone. After she retired, she moved into a rural part of Illinois, and my friend asked how she liked it. "Oh, it's OK, I guess," she said, "But there are *so* many Swedes!"

The Swedish and Norwegians have a long history of mild animosity toward one another, with each telling jokes about the other group, but their hostility is not like that between Turks and Armenians, or Germans and Poles, where the animosity resulted in genocides. It's more like the intra-Irish snarkiness about lace curtain Irish versus shanty Irish. It's unlikely that my friend's aunt's dislike of "Swedes" (these were Americans of Swedish descent) had much impact on anyone or anything (other than, perhaps, herself, since it might have meant she denied herself some friends). She wasn't in a position to deny important services to anyone, and there wasn't in her area a long history of discrimination against people with Swedish ancestry.

I mention this story because it shows one way that a common description of racism is wrong: that racism is only about what individuals do to each other. It isn't really about individuals; it's about systems. The aunt's behavior probably had little or no impact because it was almost certainly confined to just her, and she wasn't living in a region in which there were already structural inequalities that ensured people of Swedish descent faced discrimination in housing, hiring, policing, and so on.

My high school was in an area with a Spanish name (as is common in California), and so the people who founded it (in the very early seventies) decided to make the mascot something Hispanic—the Marauders. Designing the mascot was left to a student committee, and it being the very early seventies, they were unhappy about a militaristic symbol, and so voted for a drawing of someone napping under a sombrero. They didn't mean to be racist, but subversive, and they *were* subversive. Were there not a common perception of "Mexicans" (a term which is often bizarrely used to refer to people from anywhere in South and Central America, as well as Cuba) as lazy, this would simply have been a subversive joke. But there is that perception, and it has real consequences, so it was racist. (And it took me far too long to realize that.)

Stereotyping isn't necessarily bad—it's what the stereotypes do. We can't help but stereotype—humans cannot treat each new person as entirely individual; that isn't how we think. We go into a new situation, such as a job interview with a person we don't know, for a company we googled, in a building we've never been to, in a part of town we never visit. As we drive through that part of town, we put the things we're seeing into categories. It's in a new part of town with lots of buildings, or it's in an area with abandoned buildings, or it's entirely residential. When we get there we notice that it's in a big building, or a shed in the back of someone's yard, a building with modern architecture, or an ugly building. We googled the company, and that gave us a general sense (a stereotype) about the company—it fits the category of a profitable established company, a startup, or a family business. When we get there, the person is friendly or cold, in a suit, in a t-shirt and jeans, organized or disorganized. Humans reason by putting new experiences into categories established by previous experience. We can't reason without stereotyping.

Stereotyping is harmful depending on where the stereotype came from (is it an accurate generalization of the group), whether it's used to rationalize systemic discrimination, and if it's non-falsifiable.

If I believe that "Swedes" are all greedy, the cognitive bias of "confirmation bias" ensures that I'll notice every instance of a "Swede" doing something that might be interpreted as greedy, and I won't notice times that Norwegians are greedy (or I'll explain them away). Confirmation bias means looking for evidence that we're right; thinking rationally means looking for evidence that we're wrong.

9
Understand the Role of Privilege

A lot of white people get their hackles up when anyone talks about privilege because they think they're being told that they skidded into their situation without any work. In my experience, when the issue of privilege comes up, white people (white males, especially) start talking about whether they deserve what they have, whether they earned it. When I try to talk to people about privilege, privileged people instantly shift the question to whether they deserve what they have–they make it an identity issue, about them. That's the same move I've been saying all along is a mistake–whether you said something racist isn't a question of whether you're a racist; whether you've benefitted from privilege isn't a question of whether you're a slug who never did anything. The question of privilege isn't an all-or-nothing question.

Earlier I mentioned that we explain in-group good behavior (say, an in-group member petted a kitten) by individual agency (that person chose to pet the kitten), and deflect bad in-group behavior (an in-group member screamed at a kitten) through external factors (it didn't look like a kitten, the kitten provoked it). This way of explaining behavior is very clear, and very comfortable. It says that we live in a world we can entirely control through the choices we make and the actions we take. Privilege is such a vexed issue, not because it's anti-white (it isn't), but because it says that our outcomes aren't necessarily entirely the consequence of our own actions.

The important word is "entirely." We spend too much time in a world of false binaries–a person's politics are right or left, a media source is biased or objective, a position is emotional or logical. From time to time, I drift into various political worlds, and I can say that the people who rant and rave about the concept of "privilege" don't understand what it means. Oddly enough, they sometimes unintentionally endorse it while thinking they're arguing against it.

White supremacists (who don't always call themselves that) say that, since their ancestors worked hard for what they now have, they are entitled to special consideration. In other words, they want to walk into every situation privileged. So, they're granting that they're privileged–they just think it was earned by their ancestors. And, not uncommonly, these same white supremacists want to claim their entitled position on the basis of being descended from people whose achievements depended on the work of slaves, or whose family accumulated wealth during segregation. So, sometimes they simultaneously claim that they are entitled to things that their ancestors achieved through slavery and segregation *and* they are not accountable for slavery or segregation. Either they're benefitting from slavery and segregation, or they aren't.

People will sometimes say that "privilege" is a nonsense term, which just shows a failure to try to understand it, since we all endorse the notion–people walk into a situation with different levels of power that can enable them to get their way. A parent can set a bedtime for a child, but children don't get to set bedtimes for adults. A boss can insist that reports be written a particular way, regardless of what subordinates want to do. A ref can eject a player from a game with very little question; it's very rare that a player has managed to get a ref pulled from a game.

I once wrote and posted something that I'd written for a scholarly conference about how we culturally frame angry women. It got shared somewhere else, and a white male chastised me for writing something that didn't make him feel included, that didn't respond to his ideas about the issue. I pointed out that he wasn't part of my audience, but, he said (and I'm not kidding) women should always include men in their audience, since social change will require the approval of men.

That is privilege.

There is a website that has the motto along the lines of "by Black people for Black people," and they regularly get email from white people saying that they don't feel included.

That is privilege.

Privilege is thinking that you and your concerns have to be front and center for everyone else. Privilege is only partially about race.

I started the game of life with a pretty good hand. Does that mean I never worked for what I have achieved? Of course not. I worked hard. I still do. And I was lucky. But, had I been born Black (or working class, with a disability, or various other disadvantages I didn't face) I probably wouldn't be where I am. I would certainly have had to work harder to get here.

To say that I have a lot of privilege isn't some claim in an all-or-nothing way of thinking about achievement–that I either worked or didn't work for what I have.

An analogy I really like (modified from the sci-fi author John Scalzi) is that privilege is what happens in a game.* Scalzi uses the example of a computer game (in which you can set the challenge level to easy), but it might be useful to think about it as more like a role-playing game (in which you roll dice for various qualities you have) or even a card game (in which you start with a particular hand). Some people start with advantages–you've got the game set on easy, you rolled high, you started with a great hand. But, you still have to play well to win. You still have to work.

People like me who started with a lot of advantages–with a lot of privilege–aren't guaranteed a good outcome, and we face

---

* See "Straight White Male: The Lowest Difficulty Setting There Is," whatever.scalzi.com.

obstacles. Asking that we check our privilege isn't saying that we are people who have never faced any obstacles, but simply that we are looking at a situation from our perspective, and it might not be the most relevant perspective. For instance, when I went to graduate school, it wasn't possible–let alone necessary–to buy a personal computer, tuition was low, housing close to campus was available and affordable. Therefore, although the stipend was also low, it was possible to make it through the program with very little debt. Since I came from a family that could completely pay for my undergraduate education, I started graduate school with no debt at all. That was all privilege. That I was so privileged means that any advice I might now give to students considering graduate school is worth less than the advice of someone closer to them in experience. Were I to forget that my experience was so privileged, and gave advice to someone without that privilege, it would be perfectly reasonable for them to tell me to check my privilege. They would be telling me that my advice isn't relevant to them. And they would be right.

Sometimes someone telling us that we should check our privilege is a way of saying that they think our judgment about something is so limited by our privilege that they intend to ignore our position entirely. That's a prerogative we all have when it comes to conversation–dismissing what the other person says. Someone saying out loud that they're dismissing our opinion doesn't change much–that's what they were going to do anyway. I'm often asked what we should do if someone tells us to check our privilege, and the answer is: Check our privilege. If it isn't immediately obvious how we're letting privilege limit our understanding, then we can ask for clarification–which someone may or may not give.

Ijeoma Oluo says, "Privilege, in the social justice context, is an advantage or a set of advantages that you have that others do not."

She argues that "check your privilege" means working to understand "the full impact of these advantages and disadvantages in order to move toward real change in our society and ourselves."*

I'm polite to the police. So are many of the people who get shot. It isn't about being polite.

---

* See pp. 59–60 in *So You Want to Talk About Race*

10
Don't Make the Discussion About You

Many years ago, I was at a small gathering of women, and one of the women launched into a tirade about how Jewish women are pushy. I said, since I don't know any better than to engage someone like that, "That seems kind of anti-Semitic to me." She said, "Oh, you're just saying that because you're Jewish." I said, "But I'm not Jewish." She said, "Oh, you probably are and you just don't know it."

That is a perfect example of how racism is a way of thinking, the way that racism creates its own evidence, which is then used to "support" the claim that is actually the source of the evidence. Her initial assumption was that only Jews object to anti-Semitism, because, as with the friends of mine I mentioned above who are Latina, the assumption is that only members of a group object to slurs about that group. Here's what's interesting: I disproved that assumption by objecting. But instead of admitting she was wrong, she decided I was still *really* only rejecting her obviously true (to her) claim because I was biased. But I was unknowingly biased? If only members of a "race" object to slurs about that race, why would I object since, by her argument, I didn't know I was a member of a race?

She had a belief about Jews *and about who objects to racism*, and she scrambled to find "reasons" to support her beliefs even when those beliefs contradicted one another. And that is how we all, in our worst moments, argue. She was scrambling to find reasons to support her beliefs rather than being open to being wrong.

We are all her. We are all people who categorize others, who walk into every situation with expectations based on our beliefs about how things work, and who scramble (sometimes incoherently) to find a way to make contradicting information support what we already believe.

As I said earlier, I've long tried to talk to people (and think) about racism, and I've spent far too much time reading racist books, speeches, and pamphlets. And no one calls themselves racist. Even the Nazis, whose genocidal plans about various groups were thoroughly racist, rationalized their genocides on the grounds that Jews were politically dangerous. Thus, someone standing at a ditch shooting people could sincerely believe he wasn't engaged in a racist action. He was killing political enemies.

That you believe you aren't engaged in something racist is not a "get out of racism free" card.

Racism isn't a question of what racists do—it's a way we're all likely to think. Racism is about the stories we tell ourselves about ourselves and other groups. Racism is an unconscious way of explaining the behaviors of various people–we *think* differently about in- and out-groups. We expect bad behavior on the part of out-group members, and therefore we notice it, and when we notice it, our having noticed that bad behavior confirms our preconception that the out-group is lazy, criminal, corrupt, rude. We think that data that confirms our beliefs is proof, but data that complicates our beliefs is biased.

We perceive bad behavior on the part of an in-group differently–they aren't really in-group, they aren't representative, evidence we would think valid for condemning the out-group is irrelevant for condemning the in-group; the out-group has bad motives, but the in-group has good motives. If I'm a passionate supporter of Chester for President, and he says something I would think racist if said by his opponent (or said about my in-group), I'll explain that it wasn't racist: It was a slip of the tongue, it was a joke, it wasn't racist because it's true, you're being oversensitive, it can't have been racist because he has POC friends/relatives.

And here we are back to my hitting your car. If I said that I didn't hit your car because it was an accident, a joke, you deserved to have your car hit, you're being oversensitive, I have friends who are good drivers–you'd recognize none of that is relevant. And it's also weird–instead of talking about your car, I've essentially made the conversation about my being a good person and your not being attentive to my feelings.

I've made the conversation about me.

At the beginning of this book, I mentioned controversies on a mailing list of scholars of communication, and how the two different controversies (was that a racist comment? is that a racist process?) escalated wildly. And both those controversies ended up on the question of whether the people who were accused of saying something racist or being part of a racist process were being insulted. White people accused of being racist made the argument about their feelings. Austin Channing Brown describes the ways that discussions about race keep ending up being about white people's fragile feelings:

> If Black people are dying in the street, we must consult with white feelings before naming the evils of police brutality. If white family members are being racist, we must take Grandpa's feelings into account before we proclaim our objections to such speech. If an organization's policies are discriminatory and harmful, that can only be corrected if we can ensure white people won't feel bad about the change.*

White people making the issue about whether white people feel OK about this conversation rather than whether white people have been

---

* See page 89, *I'm Still Here: Black Dignity in a World Made for Whiteness* (New York: Convergent, 2018).

racist is about as good an example of privilege as I can imagine. We do that. We should stop doing that.

If I hit your car, and you said I hit your car, and I tried to say that you shouldn't say I hit your car because that makes me feel bad, you would call it out as the entitled jerk move it is.

11
Six Common Reasons People Say Something Is Racist

I'm saying that disagreements about race tend to go so badly because we disagree about what it means for something to be racist, while assuming we are all using the same definition. In addition, many people assume that there is an absolute binary between racist and not racist: Only racists like racist movies (or books, or candidates), racists know they're racist, and racist movies, people, books, should be banned or shunned. I'm saying that this way of thinking about something being racist makes the stakes frighteningly high, so it seems that we *must* come to an agreement. We *must* figure out who is right and who is wrong.

If we think about racism in terms of degrees of racist, and we think about racism as being about harm, then we don't necessarily have to agree. A disagreement can be useful, productive, and effective even if we don't end up agreeing about whether something is racist. In fact, because being told that something we've done (or liked) is racist can be so triggering, it can be a good choice to listen to what someone else has to say and take time to think about how we want to respond.

If we're talking about a movie I like that you think is racist, shifting away from the question of whether I'm racist would mean that we talked about the movie. What if, instead of my instantly getting defensive and defending myself and dragging out my history of anti-racist actions, I asked you, "What aspects of it do you think are racist?" That would be nice.

Let's imagine a movie, called *Chester and the Squirrels*,* which is set in the 1930s, about a writer from New York who admires Southern culture, and he wants to write a novel about the elegance of the planter class. He travels to the South, and he's invited to the homes of the wealthiest white people, where he hears appallingly racist things. He befriends an African American menial worker (a chauffeur, perhaps, or a garbage collector) who shows him the underside of that elegance, and so, in the dramatic denouement, he chews out the planter class "friends" he's made for being racist, and then goes back to New York, sadder and wiser about how thoroughly racist the South is.

I want to watch that movie, and you say, "I hate that movie–it's so effing racist." Or, perhaps, you say, "You like that movie? You're a racist."

---

* I just made this up. I've found that if I use a real example, hot cognition gets triggered, and people lose track of the point I'm trying to make because they're so set on their perception that the movie is/isn't racist.

If I want to talk about whether the movie is racist, the first thing for me to do is to ask you why you think the movie is racist. (It's worth evading the question of whether I'm racist, even if your saying that really hurt my feelings, since that's the route where we end up shouting at each other.) And you might decline to say, and that's fine. You don't have to be the racist whisperer.* We can just move on to picking a different movie. You don't owe me an explanation, and you aren't my only source of information. My trying to force you into a defense of your position would not indicate my openness to discussions about race. It would be a total jerk move.

If I'm genuinely curious as to why some people think the movie is racist, I could google

---

* It also means that it's always fine to say, "I think the movie is racist, and I'd rather not watch it." If I push, you can say, "Hey, let's just have a fun evening and watch something else. I'm not saying you're an evil person–I just don't want to watch it. If you're really interested in the argument about it being racist, you can look it up, or I can send you some links." Or, you can just say, "I'd rather not watch that movie."

it, and read arguments by the smartest people I can find who are saying that the movie is racist.* I won't know if I any of those reasons are the same as yours, so I can't argue with you about it.

That's an important point. We are often presented with straw man versions of opposition arguments, and a lot of times think we know what They think, and we don't. There is rarely only one argument on each side of whether a movie is racist. For instance, while many people are aware that there are arguments about whether *To Kill a Mockingbird* is racist, they are not necessarily aware that there aren't just two positions on that. Some people argue that it's racist because it has racist epithets in it, regardless of who uses them. Some people, such as Andray Domise, have very nuanced arguments about problems with the book–not that it should be

---

* Reading in-group arguments–that is, arguments saying it isn't racist–that claim to represent the opposition arguments would be just another form of the jerk move.

banned, nor even condemned as racist, but that there are better books for teaching about racism.* Even authors who suggest it could be considered "a profoundly racist book" (Tanya Landman) have nuanced arguments, about whether the superficiality of the African American characters, simplicity of the solution, and appeal to stereotypes make it a deeply problematic book.†

I was surprised to learn from various high school teachers that some of them were told to stop teaching the book because parents complained that it was racist—these were white parents who felt the book was racist about whites. And that (surprising) array of positions on the question of the book's racism is typical of the controversies about racism—thus, I can't be certain I know what your argument is just because I think I know what "the" argument is

---

* See Andray Domise, "No, *To Kill a Mockingbird* Shouldn't Be Taught in 2018," *The Globe and Mail*, October 21, 2018.

†See Tanya Landman, "Is *To Kill a Mockingbird* a Racist Book?," *The Guardian*, October 20, 2015.

that the movie is racist. There are rarely only two positions.

In my experience, people characterize something like a movie as racist because the movie:

- is about race
- was written, produced, or directed by a total racist (or it stars one, or it's based on a novel that's racist)
- uses racist epithets
- reinforces racist stereotypes
- reinforces racist narratives (tropes)
- privileges the white experience.

So, what does the conversation look like for each of these criteria for a movie being racist?

The movie is about race, or makes any generalizations about race. In my experience, the people who argue a movie (or speech, or TV show) is racist because it mentions race are the same people who claim, "I don't see color." This conversation is very complicated, because it's really about how perception works. They don't literally mean they don't see race, so it can be helpful to point that out (such as by asking, "Are you saying you don't know what race you are? Or I am?"). What they mean is that they don't consciously make decisions on the basis of race, and, since they think racism is the *conscious* differential treatment of people on the basis of race, if we all just choose to ignore race, racism will go away.

It can be helpful to talk about systemic injustice, by, for instance, pointing out that people with African American sounding names and the same resumes as those without get fewer interviews, or African Americans get pulled over, or they have more trouble getting loans and apartments (or other examples elsewhere in this book). At that point, the conversation divides. Some people will then say something like, "Oh, well, that's because they're bad tenants," or "They commit more crime," or something else that means the person just pulled the hood out of their closet. And then you can say, "So, you do see race, after all."

But some people sincerely believe that they don't treat people differently (and maybe they don't–perhaps saints walk among us), and they see themselves as being the change they want to see in the world. With people like that, the conversation ends up being about whether we can solve societal problems by pretending they don't exist. Would poverty go away if we stopped saying the word, if we pretended it didn't exist? It wouldn't, because poverty (like racism) isn't purely the consequence of conscious decisions that individuals make, so this conversation becomes about systemic racism.

The very concept of systemic racism (or poverty) is threatening to people who believe that individuals have pure agency–that humans are capable of making any choice, and of getting any outcome if they want it enough.

People who believe in this kind of pure individual agency are also deeply threatened by the concept of privilege, since it seems to them to mean that their life is not purely a consequence of their choice; it threatens their whole system. This kind of system is an instance of what's called "the just world model." The just world model says that good things happen to good people and bad things happen to bad people–we get what we deserve in this life. The just world model significantly contributes to racism in that it prevents us from acknowledging, let alone solving, systemic racism.

The just world model is central to some people's understanding of how the world works, so we aren't going to talk them out of it in one conversation. All we can do is point out a few problems with it.

The movie was written, produced, or directed by a total racist (or was based on an admittedly racist book). This is one of those criteria that not everyone shares, and that's fine.

If we think about racism in terms of harm, then we can talk about whether the racism of the author shows up in the movie (perhaps it doesn't). Or, we can talk about whether watching the movie will put money in the pocket of a racist. But, even if it does neither of those, it might be painful for you to watch the movie. That's enough harm for us not to watch it.

The deeper question is whether something having racist origins means it's racist forever (such as clowns). There are clichés and terms that are the equivalent of clowns. "Hooligan," for instance, came from the notion that the Irish (Houlihan) were essentially criminal. Since so few people know that, using the term doesn't seem to me to be racist. Some terms or phrases can be, if not racist, then hurtful. Sayings like "sold me down the river" or "tied to the whipping post" refer to tragic practices in US slavery, although I suspect that most people who use those expressions are unaware of the implications. Enough people do know, however, so that using them is a hurtful reminder. When people use those phrases to describe experiences that are merely irritating or disappointing, it seems to me a harmful trivializing of what were actually horrific situations. It seems to me that, when pundits or political figures compare their mildly uncomfortable experience to slavery or the Holocaust, it rises to the level of racism. Having to pay taxes is sometimes frustrating, but it's nothing like slavery.*

It uses racist epithets. For some people, it might depend on which characters are using the epithets, and how the audience is supposed to respond to them. If, for instance, the only people who use the epithets are the

---

* When people describe being worried about saying or doing something racist, they often mention this specific situation–the possibility of using a term we don't realize is racist. And that situation comes up because it happens, and we feel bad when it does. Racism is so deeply interwoven into our world that of course it comes up in language, and we do use phrases and terms that are racist–I only recently found out about the racist origin of "Long time, no see." But all we can do is apologize and not use the expression again.

villains, and their use of that language signals their villainy–if we're supposed to be angered and offended by the language and the characters who use it, then I might believe that the epithets are part of the anti-racist message of the movie. This criterion gets especially complicated when it comes to older books or movies, in which some racist epithets were more common (such as World War II movies in which people have nicknames that are based on ethnic slurs). In some texts, the racist epithets are there for rhetorical effect (as people argue happens in *Heart of Darkness* or *Adventures of Huckleberry Finn*). So, we can have a conversation about what the racist epithets are doing.

Or not. As with not wanting to watch an actor you think is racist, you just might not want to watch a movie with a lot of racist epithets in it (just as you might not want to watch a movie with a lot of violence, nudity, loud explosions). We don't have to agree about the complicated question as to whether the movie is racist for using racist epithets to agree that we shouldn't watch it. If it hurts you to watch a movie like that, and we're friends, simply that it hurts you should be enough for me.

It reinforces racist stereotypes. In my experience, this criterion is complicated by the way that racist stereotypes can seem to people to be "positive." For instance, abolitionists, in an attempt to persuade people that slavery was harmful, often emphasized the childlike innocence of slaves–a stereotype that appeared "positive," but actually reinforced racist notions that African Americans were incapable of the kind of rational thinking necessary for full citizenship. While appealing to the notion of childlike and innocent African Americans may have been useful in arguing against slavery, it did tremendous harm in rationalizing denying full citizenship to African Americans. It was rhetoric, even if in service of an anti-racist agenda (something can be racist in some ways and anti-racist in others). I'm old enough to remember people in Southern California saying that people in "the South" were so wrong to be racist, because African Americans (of course, not the term they used) were good. They were, these people said, "so good with children, and have such a great sense of rhythm." Even as a child, that seemed stupid to me. Those aren't qualities actually valued by our culture. "Positive" qualities that serve to justify racist hierarchies aren't positive at all. They're racist.

This criterion about racism (it reinforces existing hierarchies by reinforcing stereotypes) is relatively straightforward when it comes to recent movies, but more complicated when it comes to older ones. *South Pacific*, after all, was banned by the South African government in 1963 and condemned on the floor of the Alabama legislature when it came out, so it must have been doing good anti-racist work.* *To Kill a*

---

* For a summary, see "'South Pacific' Banned," *The New York Times*, January 1, 1964.

Mockingbird obviously did good anti-racist work in its era, and can be admired for that, since it undercut contemporary stereotypes about Black men.

The paradox of persuasion is that the most effective way to move people to new positions is to take them from where they are to a new place. That is, to find common ground. Thus, anti-racist rhetoric might be effective precisely because it finds common ground with racists. Rhetoric that was effectively anti-racist in its era might quickly become racist in another because of that racist common ground (such as abolitionist rhetoric). There are movies that students describe having been eye-opening for them as children but later came to seem so simplistic in the presentation of racism as to be racist in effect. It seems to me sensible that we might explain racism to children with books or movies that are useful for a child's level of understanding but are harmful for adults (because the books and movies reinforce the same stereotypes–adults should, after all, have a more nuanced understanding of racism and race relations than children). *To Kill a Mockingbird* might be a good first movie about racism (although there are better), but it shouldn't be a lodestar.

There are stereotypes that wouldn't be harmful were they less common. The model minority Asian, sassy Black woman, spicy Latina, argumentative Jew, mystical indigenous person, and so on are damaging because they show up in so many movies, novels, TV shows, ads. As TV Tropes, the pop-culture wiki, says, these tropes are "stereotypical and lazy writing and people want to see minority characters given the same nuanced characterisation as anyone else."*

Sometimes these stereotypical characters are part of an overused stereotypical narrative, such as the magical minority who changes the life of a white person (the lead) with folksy wisdom, spiritual insight, selfless

* See "Sassy Black Woman," tvtropes.org

support. The lead is transformed by this nonwhite character, while that nonwhite character remains the same. Your objection to the *Chester and the Squirrels* might be that it follows exactly that stereotypical narrative. The white lead goes to the South, is enlightened by the chauffeur, and then goes back North, *without actually having improved the chauffeur's life*. The chauffeur (or garbage collector, or maid, or whatever–these sorts of movies also present African Americans as poor and uneducated) only matters insofar as they cause a change in a white person.

You might also object that the movie confirms a harmful narrative about racism–that racism is a problem in the South (and, by implication, not elsewhere), that racism was bad in the thirties (leaving aside the question of current racism), that racism is a problem of individuals who use racist epithets and openly advocate policies they know to be racist. I've argued that our understanding about racism and how it works is seriously impaired–and our discussions about racism fueled for escalation–because of precisely that explanation of racism (racism is what racist people do, and racist people know they're being racist and like it). So, *Chester and the Squirrels* confirms a harmful stereotype about racism.

Were *Chester and the Squirrels* unique, or even unusual, in its making racism about the South and about the past, and so on, then it wouldn't be as much of a problem. Were there lots of movies about racism in other parts of the country and our current era, then there wouldn't be a preexisting damaging movie narrative that the film would be reinforcing. More harm comes from the pattern.

When we're talking about this kind of racism–a movie that wouldn't be as harmful were it unique–it's helpful to keep in mind that liking the movie doesn't mean we're evil. Just as the pattern of movie-making matters, so the pattern of our own movie consumption matters. If the only movies (or TV shows, or novels) I consume are ones that rely on racial/ethnic stereotypes, then my consumption is racist in that it's going to reinforce limiting stereotypes about various groups. The solution isn't to ban *Chester and the Squirrels*, but for me to watch a wider variety of movies, and to push for a more diverse set of directors, writers, producers.

It privileges the white experience. Lots of movies are more or less from one perspective, in that we hear only or mostly about one character's internal transformations. But, if all or most movies are about the rich internal lives only of white people, then culturally we have a narrative that only white people have rich internal lives, or, perhaps, that only the feelings of white people matter. Movies, TV shows, novels, theater–these are storehouses of stories, these are the places we learn to imagine other lives. If white people only watch movies about white people, in which only white people have rich internal lives and deep transformations, then they'll have little or no empathy–let alone understanding–of the lives of others. A life spent in which only white people have interesting feelings is one that sets a person up to think that white people's feelings are the center of every interaction, the only thing that matters. Being a good human means being able to privilege the feelings of others easily and with some freqency.

There is a video series called *Every Single Word,* in which movies are edited down to the parts in the movie spoken by persons of color. To take simply one example, for all of Nancy Meyers's movies put together (she has directed, written, or produced sixteen films), every single word spoken by a person of color adds up to well under ten minutes total. That's a pattern; it's also an imagined world in which people of color are nothing more than bits of scenery for what is framed as important: white people's feelings. That's racist, even if there are no racist epithets in the movies.

If you didn't want to watch *Chester and the Squirrels* because you didn't want to watch yet one more movie all about white people feelings, that would be a legitimate complaint because there are so many movies on exactly that subject. Were there not so many movies about it, were it not the dominant movie experience, I might be less persuaded.

Even if you persuade me that the movie is racist, that doesn't necessarily mean you have persuaded me (let alone that you think) that every copy should be burned and anyone who likes it should be shamed. It might be mixed–anti-racist in some ways, and racist in others. It might be an interesting cultural artifact, showing how people thought about race at a particular moment. It might have dog whistle racism when there no longer any dogs trained to hear that whistle (like the clowns). Whether something is racist is a preliminary conversation to what we're going to do about it.

The example I've used–a conversation between the two of us about a movie we might choose to watch–is high stakes if and only if we choose to make it so (e.g., if we make the issue whether I am a terrible person). Some disagreements are high stakes, such as when one of the parties can force the other to watch the movie. That's the situation we have when it comes to arguments about whether books should be taught (that is, *required*) in school.

But here, too, the same principles apply: It's about patterns. I had a student who came from an area that had a strong Black middle class, and she grew up in a school with a lot of readings by Black authors. In high school, she told me, they read *Adventures of Huckleberry Finn*, and talked in class about whether it was racist. She didn't think it was a particularly troubling book because Jim was just a character, and he didn't represent Black men. When she came to a university with a very small number of nonwhite students, she started to meet white people who didn't know many (or, in some cases, any) Black men, and whose secondhand knowledge was limited to Martin Luther King Jr.'s

"I Have a Dream" speech (which they liked) and Malcolm X (whom they feared) and Jim. Suddenly, she told me, she saw the representation of Jim as much more damaging, and the book as much more racist than she had. It was the same book, but with a different, and more racist, impact. Just to be clear: I'm not saying that she was wrong about it when she read it in high school. I'm saying, as was she, that it had a different impact because, in a world with so few representations of African American men, the few that do exist have a powerful impact.

When it comes to teaching, we have a tendency to argue about individual texts, rather than talk about the curriculum. We don't bring diversity to a curriculum if white students only read the same one or two African American authors, especially if they read the same texts by those one or two authors over and over. If something like *To Kill a Mockingbird* is presented to students as a novel about which they might disagree, then its low-key racism is less of a problem than if students are required to express admiration for it.

12
Racism Isn't About White People's Feelings

I want to circle back to something mentioned earlier. Berry and Sobieraj argued that conservatives are afraid of being called racist, and that may be a true summary of their survey data–but that feeling is not because only conservatives get accused of doing or saying something racist. The notion that "liberals" believe no liberal is racist and all conservatives are is a canard promoted by, oddly enough, *conservative* media. Tim Wise's description of his life as a white anti-racist activist has several instances of people accusing him of being racist, and his deciding they were right; Ibram X. Kendi's *How to Be an Antiracist* describes racism that operates in "liberal" spaces, as does Ijeoma Oluo's *So You Want to Talk About Race.*

We will all do something racist at some point, or fail to do something to ameliorate racism—we'll tolerate racist hiring practices, ignore the disparate racial consequences of a policy that benefits us, overlook racist practices or policies in our communities, smile blandly at a racist joke, or perhaps even make a racist joke. At that moment, when we want to be better, it's important that we not make the objects of our racism the angels who will save us. People of color were not put on earth to help white people be less racist; they have lives. No one should try to force an apology on someone who doesn't want to hear it, who might not be ready to forgive, or who might not even be thinking in terms of forgiveness and guilt. White people shouldn't expect that nonwhite friends, acquaintances, or coworkers have nothing better to do than explain racism to them, that they are the only source of information. I've included a list of useful books, and there are numerous websites and blogs with their own lists.

Most important, we shouldn't rely entirely on in-group media to tell us everything we need to know about anything, let alone about race. We are in a world in which many of us have strong opinions on issues about which we are actually uninformed, and sometimes misinformed, and that's a bad combination. There are a lot of institutional, systemic, and policy issues related to race, and they're complicated: the school-to-prison pipeline, funding of education and infrastructure, cultural appropriation, employment law. If we have a strong opinion on any issue, and we've never looked at the best arguments for other points of view, we're not really informed, just opinionated.

13
Key Things to Remember in the Heat of the Moment

In short, if someone says we're racist, we need to:

- Try to figure out why they said that (if possible, ask them), being open to the possibility that they're right.
- If it's that we've said, done, or liked something racist, then make the discussion about that thing, *not about our feelings.*
- Try to understand what definition of racism/racist they're using, and, if possible, try to reach agreement as to that definition.

- Understand that we may strongly believe that we aren't racist—that some group of people really is more criminal, dangerous, terrorist, and so on—because we're in an informational bubble.
- Actively try to understand the counterarguments and counter-information to what we believe.
- Don't feel that we have to clear ourselves of the accusation of being racist, or that this conversation has to end with everyone in agreement.
- Don't "sea lion." Sea lioning, based on a meme of a sea lion who photobombs, is insisting that the person persuade us; it's making us the center of the other person's life—we have the internet; we can look things up.
- Take time to think about it, talk to others, read things outside of our informational bubble—begin with the premise that they're right, and see if we can confirm that what we said or did was racist.

If we are often told that we have said, done, or liked something racist, maybe we should try being less racist.

If we're trying to tell someone that they've said or done something racist, then we should:

- Try to figure out if the person cares about having said or done something racist.
- If they don't, and whatever they've said or done was in a very public place, then it might be worth just pointing out that it was racist, giving a few links (if it's social media), and walking away.
- If you think they did it without knowing (such as using a term that a lot of people might not know is racist), then point it out privately and kindly.
- If you think they are repeating something that they got from their media enclave, then (if it's social media) give links or explain the problem.
- If you've been to this rodeo many times, and know they will refuse to look at

information from outside of the media that tells them what they want to hear, then set boundaries ("I don't want to talk about that–here, have more pie").*

- If they like making racist "jokes" or they're the kind of coward/bully who expresses racist opinions but then claims you're the one in the wrong for not having a sense of humor, put the discomfort on them (the Captain Awkward blog has a lot of good advice about this). They'll try to shift the argument away from what they did to what you are, and refuse to take the burden of proof.

---

*I find it endlessly fascinating that people who refuse to look at anything that disagrees with them–that presents a different political perspective–do so on the grounds that it must be "biased," since it's critical of their position. They don't object to biased media–that's all they consume. It seems to me that it's an admission that their beliefs are too fragile to be tested. Of course, I'm not saying that people have to read *everything* with which we disagree, but we should be willing to look at the strongest counterarguments.

- Avoid sea lioning. If you think the person is insisting that you prove to them that they're wrong, and they're doing so in bad faith, then give them some links, and walk away.

Given that we're in a racist culture, it's almost certain that we will say and do racist things, and it can hurt to be told that we have done so. But, if we do a lot of racist things, and if people often criticize us for being racist, then one way to reduce the amount that we're hurt by being told we're racist is to worry less about our feelings, and more about whether we might have said or done something racist.

14
A Final Note

At the beginning of the book, I mentioned that there are times when it's useful to consider whether someone is racist. On the whole, I'm saying we should keep the issue on actions and harm rather than identity. If I hit your car, the issue isn't whether I'm a good driver, but the damage I did and how I can undo it. But, after a while, whether I'm a good driver *would* become the issue–if I hit a lot of cars, if I have a lot of accidents, you might decide I'm genuinely a bad driver. You might try to talk me into taking lessons, but you also might just decide you aren't getting into the car with me, or, if you do, you aren't letting me drive.

There are also people who are deliberately racist, and very little of what I've said in this book will enable you to talk reasonably with them. It won't help you disagree with them because they're not able to engage in useful disagreement (sometimes about anything, in my experience). We can figure out who they are because they keep saying, doing, and endorsing racist things, sometimes claiming they don't mean to be racist, and sometimes openly advocating racism. Don't let them drive the car.

Suggested Reading

Moustafa Bayoumi. *How Does It Feel to Be a Problem?: Being Young and Arab in America*. New York: Penguin Books, 2008.

How Does It Feel to Be a Problem? has seven chapters, each of which focuses on a young Arab American and their experiences before, during, and after 9/11. This book is particularly useful for readers who think that all Arab Americans are Muslim, let alone all terrorists.

Austin Channing Brown. *I'm Still Here: Black Dignity in a World Made for Whiteness*. New York: Convergent Books, 2018.

Brown's book, like many of the recommended books, interweaves her personal experiences with reflections on race and racism–in this case, particularly the challenges of being a

Black woman. The book is especially helpful for understanding how racist actions can arise in communities of people who genuinely think we aren't being racist.

Ibram X. Kendi. *How to Be an Antiracist.* New York: One World, 2019.

Kendi, whose earlier book *Stamped from the Beginning,* is a thorough and smart history of the impact of slavery in US history, mixes scholarly research, personal narrative, and reflection to argue persuasively for the goal of active anti-racism rather than non-racism.

Aaron J. Layton. *Dear White Christian: What Every White Christian Needs to Know About How Black Christians See, Think, & Experience Racism in America.* PCA Committee on Discipleship Ministries, 2017.

Layton's book is a good first book about racism for conservative Christians who believe society is post-racist, because he spends so much time emphasizing shared values (such as kindness and compassion).

Trevor Noah. *Born a Crime: Stories from a South African Childhood.* New York: Random House, 2019.

Noah's book is a good place to start reading about racism for someone skeptical about racism in the US because it's mostly about his experience growing up in South Africa–US readers can come to understand issues about racism without feeling defensive.

Viet Thanh Nguyen, ed. *The Displaced: Refugee Writers on Refugee Lives.* New York: Harry N. Abrams, 2018.

A powerful collection of nineteen short pieces written by people with widely varying experiences of threat, escape, and refuge that complicates and humanizes our understanding of refugees.

Ijeoma Oluo. *So You Want To Talk About Race.* New York: Seal Press, 2018.

Oluo's book is especially helpful for people who think that progressive politics are inherently anti-racist, as she accurately describes how people can be racist even when we think we aren't.

Adam Rutherford. *How to Argue With a Racist: What Our Genes Do (and Don't) Say About Human Difference.* New York: The Experiment, 2020.

Rutherford, a geneticist, cogently and persuasively shows that any attempt to ground our current understandings of race in biology or genetics is nonsense.

Anton Treuer. *Everything You Wanted to Know About Indians But Were Afraid to Ask.* St. Paul, MN: Borealis Books, 2012.

Treuer has collected the questions he's been frequently asked when he does presentations and workshops about Native Americans and provides cogent and helpful answers for the most recurrent ones.

Damon Tweedy. *Black Man in a White Coat: A Doctor's Reflections on Race and Medicine.* New York: Macmillan, 2016.

Tweedy's book is another one that might be a comfortable place for conservatives to start, since he responds compassionately and carefully to many of the concerns they raise about personal responsibility, affirmative action, and the goal of color-blind judgment.

Tim Wise. *White Like Me: Reflections on Race from a Privileged Son*. Berkeley, CA: Soft Skull Press, 2011.

Wise describes privilege thoughtfully and usefully, and the book is particularly useful for thinking about how class and race intersect.